THE NEW INVESTING MATRIX

The Updated and Definitive Investment Guide

Wayne Walker

Contents

Disclaimer

The advice and strategies contained in this book are based on my personal investment choices experiences and opinions, and may not be appropriate for your situation.

INTRODUCTION

n this book we will explore investing in the most comprehensive way possible. The goal is to systematically create an investment plan that goes beyond traditional investing strategies. The "classics" are not thrown away but will be looked at from different angles. This updated investment matrix, I feel secure in stating, will provide readers with a new way to look at investing. As I often write in my books, freedom is the goal and there are many, many ways to get there, which include using new asset classes. In the coming pages you (the reader) will be also considered as an asset class. Everyone knows of stocks, bonds, and so forth, and we will examine them, but we also need to look at the most important asset class ... you.

THE MOST IMPORTANT ASSET CLASS
YOU

You

Yes, you! We begin with the most important asset class. No need to worry, obviously we will get to the "real stuff" of capital market assets, but in the investing matrix for 2021 and beyond, to ignore yourself as an asset class in my opinion is a mistake. If you the person as an asset is not developing or protected, then the other traditional assets are at risk. For those who have read my other books, you know that I like to get to the point without it taking hundreds of pages and I will not let you down.

Sleep

You need it. Forget the fake macho nonsense talk about working month after month on three or four hours sleep during a twenty-four-hour cycle. Notice that I mentioned cycle and not each night; this is because I recognize that we are all different and run on different systems. I am a hopeless night owl, and in my world, working until two or three in the morning is the norm for my colleagues and me. However, for others that is not the case, a close friend of mine is up daily at 7 a.m. or earlier; luckily we do not share the same house. What we can all agree on is that during a twenty-four-hour cycle it is important to get enough sleep, ideally seven to nine hours. Since we are not robots you can, for example, take seven hours in one shot and later one hour of napping, if your job or business allows for this. Ensuring that you get enough sleep is a great way to protect asset number one, you. Being more alert allows you to analyze the other asset classes better and probably makes you a friendlier person to be with.

Intermittent Fasting (IF)

Intermittent fasting (IF) is one of the best things that I have done for my personal life. IF is where there are windows of time that you eat and times that you do not. For example, you do not eat between 9 p.m. and 1 p.m. (the next day) and you eat during the other hours. This version is called 16/8 in the IF world, but there are other methods. Keep in mind this is not a diet, so you are not on or off it. This is a lifestyle plus eating pattern. Since it is not a diet, you can eat what you want in between, ideally healthy, but that is up to you. Over time, what most people experience after beginning is a noticeable drop in body fat and increased energy. Those were the results for me. In addition, my life became easier because I only deal with preparing two meals a day instead of the traditional three or four. I am not a dietician or doctor so this *not* medical advice. The studies and results of people from around the world that practice IF are easy to fact check with a simple search on the Internet.

Foreign languages

Learning a foreign language is one of the best gifts that you can give yourself. I always love a good debate, but this is one topic that we can skip the debate on because the benefits are so overwhelming. Languages can increase your personal, career, or business value. This tip is more for people in countries that are known for being resistant to learning other languages. In Europe, where I live most of the year, and especially in Scandinavia, it is common to speak two or three languages fluently. I speak three languages (English, Spanish, Danish), plus one dialect.

Personally, I can clearly point to several business, personal, and romantic opportunities that have presented themselves because of my foreign language skills. This is truly a skill that increases the value of the asset class *you* and it is fun.

Continuous learning

We close the asset class of you with one of my favorite hobbies, which is ongoing learning. I believe most adults are aware that learning never actually stops. What we learn in schools, universities, and so on is just the base or platform that we use for further development. I remember at my own graduations I was always reminded by my parents that the moment was not the end but the beginning. They were right as usual.

This ongoing learning could be in the form of a new certification like a real estate license or just a private wish, for example, taking a flying lesson. For myself I get coaching on areas that I want to develop further. Obviously, what you learn is up to you but the point is to be alive while you are alive. I saw my father who upon his passing in his eighties was always taking a class of some kind. I have no scientific proof for it, but I noticed that compared to some of his peers the mental issues that often accompany the elderly, like memory loss, certainly had little to no effect on him.

INVESTING OVERVIEW

Clarify goals

Now that we have covered the asset class of you, it is time to move toward the world of asset classes that are tradable. While *you* as an asset class is the most valuable, the majority of people, unless they are a professional athlete, are not too crazy about being traded.

We will cover a range of topics, but before beginning our journey, we must have a clear goal. This is your moment to determine what the goal is for you. We all want to make money, but what is your focus or goal? Is it capital preservation, income, or capital appreciation? Depending on your selection, different asset classes and strategies will receive greater emphasis. It should also not be a surprise that your goals are dependent on your position in life and personal circumstances. A twenty-five-year-old new graduate and a sixty-two-year-old widow probably would have drastically different needs.

Verify your risk tolerance

Whether you are trading or investing, your risk tolerance must be established before pulling the trigger on an investment. Would a drop in the value of your investments make you lose sleep? Before deciding which investments are right for you, you need to know how much risk you are willing to assume. That level of risk, as mentioned before, depends heavily on where you are in life: the new graduate, mid-career professional, a widow, and so on.

Do you prefer rock climbing to reading a nice novel in your backyard? Investors often find that their lifestyle and investment risk tolerance do *not* match up. You can have the widow who loves skydiving but her goal, investment-wise, is capital preservation.

Selecting investments

Before choosing the investments that will become a part of your investment portfolio, you will allow yourself to be guided by the concepts of asset allocation and diversification. In asset allocation you balance risk/reward by diversifying among the different asset classes. By diversifying, you avoid exposing your portfolio to unnecessary risk. We will return to these topics and explore deeper as we progress.

Emotions

Controlling emotions is one of the most challenging tasks for many investors, so challenging that books have been written just on this topic alone. Even professionals struggle with it at times; it is not unheard of that some banks and investment houses have mental health staff just for their traders and fund managers.

As much as possible, you must avoid allowing fear or greed to inflate your losses or limit your profits. Any investor should expect and be comfortable with a certain amount of short-term fluctuations in their portfolios without going into panic mode.

Greed can lead an investor to hold an asset too long in the hope of an increase in value even as the price continues to fall over an extended period of time. Fear on the other hand can make an investor sell an investment prematurely or prevent him or her from selling a clear investment loser. Obviously, if your portfolio gives you sleepless nights then it's best to have a talk with your investment advisor.

Review and adjust

The final step in your investment journey is to review your portfolio. Once you have established an allocation strategy, you might find that your asset weightings have changed over the course of a quarter or year.

Selecting an investment advisor

The right advisor for you depends a lot on the amount of time you are willing to spend on your investments. Some people see investing as a hobby and want to be deeply involved, for others it is a chore to avoid. Your choice of advisor depends on how you assess yourself. Many institutions offer different levels of attention; often it depends on the value of your portfolio. Some people select someone independent of the institution that they have their investments with but that is a personal decision.

EQUITY VALUE INVESTING

Equities

E quities, also referred to as stocks, shares, or securities, are typically the most common way to enter the world of investing for many people. Even if they do not buy individual stocks on their own, they often times have exposure through their pension funds.

There are risks involved with any stock, but you do have the benefit of potential capital appreciation and income in the form of dividends depending on the stock. Since these are public companies, you can easily find information about them in order to make an analysis.

Value Investing

The important principle of value investing is to find companies trading below their real or inherent value. Two professors at Columbia University first presented the strategy in the 1930s and since then many others have applied their interpretation of the strategy.

Investors seek out stocks with solid fundamentals: cash flow, earnings, dividends, and so forth. The companies should be *incorrectly* valued by the market and have good potential to increase in value. In plain terms, these stocks are trading at a bargain, and will increase in value when the market corrects this valuation error.

Not junk but real value

Some new practitioners of value investing misinterpret the strategy as simply buying stocks that are falling in price since they are in theory now inexpensive. An example of this could be that stock AB has been trading at $100 per share and it suddenly falls to $78. This drop does not automatically qualify stock AB as a candidate for value investing. The only thing we know at this point is that the company is trading at a lower price. In fact, the drop in price of stock AB could be a reflection of real problems in the company.

True value investors will do in-depth analysis to discover companies that are cheap given the *fundamentals* of the company. Therefore, if a stock falls from $100 to $78, to appear on the value investing radar, the company must have the fundamentals or intrinsic worth of more than $78. What we are paying attention to is the actual share price in relation to the intrinsic value. This should not be confused with comparing the current price to historic share prices.

The Formula:

Intrinsic Value = Current Earnings x (8.5 + 2 x Expected Annual Growth Rate)
The growth figure that should be expected over the next seven to ten years.

Practical application of value investing

The shining example of value investing concepts applied can be seen with Warren Buffet and what he has done with Berkshire Hathaway. His application of the strategy has produced thousands of percent's return. Berkshire typically beats the S&P 500's performance by a noticeable margin.

A different approach

Value investors see a stock as a way through which a person becomes part or full owner of a company. They buy or invest in a company not just a stock. They expect to make their profits from their ownership of a quality company that produces long-term profits. This is in significant contrast to the average investor who is often more focused on short-term price movements.

The value investor's focus is on the underlying stock value and not the short-term daily market fluctuations. Short-term movements according to the value investing strategy are of minor significance in the long run.

Where can you find value stocks?

Value stocks can be found in just about every market available, for example, NYSE, DAX, and many others around the globe. You can also find them in a variety of industries, including technology and finance just to name a few.

Many investors in their search for value investing candidates begin in industries that have experienced recent negative market overreactions. This can be in response to news or just short-term changes in tastes. For example, the energy industry, which has a cyclical nature, offers opportunities during periods of undervaluation. A company dropping to new lows may be a sign to add it to your portfolio, but remember the low price or cheapness must be relative to the intrinsic value.

Not all agree

There is not universal agreement on the merits of value investing. There is disagreement from the efficient market theory believers. They hold the view that a stock's price reflects all relevant information. It should come as no surprise that value investors disagree on this assessment of the market. They believe, as you now know, there are inefficiencies in the market that are only waiting to be discovered. Value investing is not the flashy attention-getting way to evaluate stocks but few can argue about its results when applied correctly.

BONDS

Getting started

Many people have heard the word *bond* but not all know what it means, so we will have a short refresher. A bond is nothing more than a loan. Just as you and I need money so do governments and companies. The challenge facing both governments and companies is that the amount of funds they need is more than what most banks are willing to lend. This is why governments and others resort to issuing bonds to potential investors.

The organization selling the bond is referred to as the issuer and the investor is the one lending the money. The investor obviously expects something in return for lending his or her money and is compensated by the issuer in the form of interest payments. The interest rate is sometimes called the coupon.

Bonds are classified as fixed-income securities in the sense that you know exactly how much you will get back if you hold them until the maturity date (the date that the issuer has to return the amount borrowed).

Bonds and stocks: the practical differences

A stock allows you to be part owner of a company; in contrast, when investing in bonds it makes you a *creditor* since bonds are debt. Being a creditor does have several important advantages. One of them is, in the case of bankruptcy, bondholders are paid before shareholders. Bondholders, by the way, do not get the pleasure of sharing in the profits.

Why bonds?

Investors often look to bonds because they are generally less risky than stocks, but they normally offer lower returns when compared over the long term. The key word here is *normally*, because bonds can also be both risky and deliver a higher return depending on the class of bonds.

Bonds are appropriate when you do not have an appetite for the volatility of the stock market. There are several situations where bonds are the preferred asset class. The first is retirement, where persons are normally living off some form of fixed income. Most retirees do not have the option of losing their principal or base investments. They rely on this base to pay their day-to-day bills. So for them, bonds are a better option.

Another scenario where bonds are preferred is anyone with a short time horizon. A common example is young parents looking to buy a home within a year. We can agree that stocks provide the opportunity for higher growth, but the new parents cannot risk losing money in the near future. Fixed income is therefore the preferred vehicle for their situation.

Types of bonds

We begin with those issued by a government. These types of bonds are generally considered safe, but there are levels of safety. Those issued by the US government – for example, treasury bonds – are safe by market standards. Securities issued by developing countries are often classified as less safe due to the higher risk of default. From my experience, debts issued by developing countries have to be evaluated on a case-by-case basis because some are rated incorrectly.

Corporations can also issue bonds just as they do stocks. They range from short to long-term in terms of time frame. The market assumes that corporations have a higher default risk than a government and as such expect higher yields. The higher the credit quality of the company, the lower the interest rate they will offer to pay. Therefore, for a company, getting and maintaining a good rating is important. There is a class of corporates known as junk bonds and these carry high risk and high yield.

Investment grades

Investment Grade Bonds: AAA, AA, A, BBB

Non-Investment Grade Bonds: BB, CCC, CC, D

CRYPTOCURRENCY INVESTING

Cryptocurrencies, also called cryptos, as an asset class are not part of the traditional investment mix but they should be. They qualify because as an asset class they do not correlate with other assets, for example, stocks or commodities. They can also serve as a hedge to your other investments.

We will begin with a look at Bitcoin and move on to some of the others. This is not an opinion piece or how I personally feel about them; it is simply to answer the question "will they add value to a diversified portfolio?" The answer is a clear yes. The market returns of Bitcoin, when compared to stocks, are astonishingly in favor of Bitcoin. For those who still hold the view that this is a fad, or will just go away, the facts to date are not in your favor. Here are some examples.

Bitcoin's many "deaths"

Bitcoin has "died" 150+ times. Below are just a few of the wildly inaccurate predictions of Bitcoin's demise.

- August 11, 2013 "Why Bitcoin Is Doomed To Fail" – moneygeek | $93.43
- November 16, 2013 "Bitcoin is a Joke" – Business Insider | $433.57
- May 4, 2017 "The Beginning of the End for Bitcoin" – Daily Reckoning | $1541.90
- July 12, 2017 "Bitcoin acceptance is virtually zero and shrinking" – Yahoo Finance | $2,410.55

Some reality

Source: Python Signals

What is it?

Bitcoin is a decentralized digital currency (a digital asset). It is not a tangible asset but a digital one. For the few who might still be in doubt, these are not actual coins that you can touch. No government owns it. You can transfer money quickly without governments or banks for a low fee. In its base form it is a very secure public ledger (kind of a spreadsheet). Before money, there were ledgers. This is how primitive societies kept track of who had and did what.

Cryptocurrencies, as many say, are a natural evolution in the history of money, from bartering to coins to paper money to digital.

Secure?

What if someone or some group hacked the ledger? Even if 40%–49% were hacked, the majority would have the correct info (the ledger is decentralized). As long as the majority of the ledgers agree, the transaction is valid. If some entity tried for a 51% (majority) attack, you should be aware that an attack of this magnitude would require funds in the area of $500 million to carry out. In addition, an attack of this size would be noticed relatively quickly by the network.

Cryptocurrencies (besides Bitcoin): What do they do?

For the people who are still in awe of the amazing price movements upward that we have seen across many of the cryptocurrencies, the question that I receive the most from students and others is "what do they do?" Bitcoin of course gets the spotlight, but for the other cryptos most people are lost. Let us have a look at the more popular coins and later some thoughts on the market movements.

Ethereum (ETH) – Programmable contracts

Bitcoin (BTC) – Moving money, settling transactions, a digital asset

Dash (DASH) – Key feature is privacy

Litecoin (LTC) – Similar to Bitcoin but faster

Ripple (XRP) – Enterprise payment settlement network

The reality

The volatility we have seen with cryptocurrencies, Bitcoin, for example, was more severe in the past. Cryptos like other markets can actually go down; this point seemed like a new idea to some. When we were having the run-up with Bitcoin from $10,000 to over $19,000, faster than even the biggest fan could have imagined, the downside was forgotten. The reduction in the early hype has helped to mature the market to the point that it is now a legitimate asset class. If I wrote this ten years ago it would have provoked nothing but laughs.

Liquidity

A recent report showed that 50% of trading activity is received from just five cryptos: Ethereum, Bitcoin, Litecoin, Ripple and Bitcoin Cash. This should serve as a warning for those investors who want to maintain liquidity. Many cryptos have less than $10,000 in trading volume, something to avoid in any portfolio.

What should you really have in your crypto portfolio?

Select a few and get to know them well. As you can imagine, no investor normally has exposure to fifty different coins at a time. Most people begin crypto investing by investing in the most well-known ones, for example, Bitcoin and Ethereum. After a while, you can begin to expand your crypto universe as you get a better understanding of how they move.

Frankly, the hype around cryptos needed a vacation for the long-term good of cryptocurrencies. I believe that we are finally getting to that point. I am well aware many people have had their accounts take a few knockout blows. To be honest some have given up on cryptos altogether. The majority of the departing crypto investors are those who refused or neglected to get some training or qualified advice before diving in. I have often stressed in my other books the importance of diversification. This is an important concept with all asset classes, but with cryptos it goes from good to have to *must have*. This diversification concept is nothing magical or some deep secret. Just having a knowledge of basic investing principles along with technical analysis would have helped many with their strategy and especially their mindset.

The portfolio

What I would consider to include in a 2020 and beyond portfolio are Bitcoin, Ethereum, Ripple, Tether, Litecoin, EOS, and Bitcoin Cash. They are selected from my principle that investors should have a diverse portfolio of cryptos and only invest in those with good liquidity (by crypto standards). All the selected are in the top fifteen in terms of market capitalization.

Both the new and more experienced crypto enthusiast should be aware of the unique features of the individual coin. Each crypto asset has its distinct features in terms of market behavior. We have also seen that altcoins have their own price movement stories. Altcoins are the alternative currencies that have sprung up based on the idea and/or basic code of Bitcoin.

It is no longer valid to say, as was said in the past, that whatever Ethereum or Bitcoin do in the market the other coins will react with similar price movements. For example, a recent decline in Bitcoin did not lead to an equivalent drop for many altcoins. On the contrary, several have increased in value.

REAL ESTATE

Real estate is the asset class where the less complicated that you keep it the better off you are. My view on real estate is if you buy, you should plan to live there for at least five years. Yes, there are people flipping homes on reality TV shows, but the reality is often not as glamourous.

I have owned an apartment and homes in three different regions of the world (Europe, the Caribbean, and the United States). From this global experience, any property that I would buy now would be investment properties that I can rent out. Owning properties have so many hidden cost, taxes, repairs, and so on, that unless you intend to live there for a long time you should make it a business and invest in rental properties.

Let us have a look at some of the different ways to enter the market.

Room rentals

By far the easiest way to enter real estate is renting out a room in your current residence. The important point here is to make an honest self-assessment to establish if you can deal with having to share space with a stranger and all the challenges that it brings. Some try the Airbnb type model at first to test out their tolerance on a short-term almost risk-free basis.

REITs

REITs (Real Estate Investment Trusts) are a way to invest in real estate without owning any actual physical property. They are sometimes compared to mutual funds and are known to pay good dividends. The companies behind them usually own a portfolio of properties that includes hotels, office buildings, and apartments. Some REITs are traded publicly, others are not. I suggest that you as a private investor keep to exchange-traded funds because of the better liquidity. Profits are great but if you are unable to collect them due to liquidity issues then it is a sad joke.

Rental property investing

Many people enter this area of investing initially by buying a place bigger than what they have a need for and then renting out the extra space. This type of deal can usually leave the investor with a profit after accounting for all the expenses. From here you can graduate to other properties and replicate the process, but now you do not live at the property, the residence is 100% rental. This is something that I am in the middle of doing in Southern Europe.

This form of investment does require some homework as always. You will need to know what the rental market is like and what the projections for the area are. Similar to other investments, you need to make failure survivable by not overextending yourself with credit in order to acquire the property. Those that I am looking at are where I buy the properties on an all-cash offer. This is done to secure a better price from the sellers.

CAPITAL MARKETS ASSETS ALLOCATION

O ur journey has arrived at the blind spot that many investors have, and that is optimal asset allocation. The focus will be on your capital market assets and not on, for example, real estate. The question that must be answered immediately is "what is asset allocation?" It is the strategy that guides you in the process of dividing your assets among the different asset classes. Your aim as an investor is to maximize returns while keeping risk at the lowest level possible. Simple, but not easy.

Assets risk-reward profiles

To achieve the goal of maximum returns at the lowest possible risk requires that you know the risk-reward profile of the various asset classes.

Money Markets: Debt securities, very liquid, and have maturities of less than a year.

Fixed-Income (Bonds): Pays a regular and fixed amount of interest. Some also pay interest at maturity. They typically have a lower level of volatility when compared to stocks. However, they are not totally risk-free because there is always the risk of default.

Developing (Emerging) Markets: Stocks from developing countries. Generally have the potential for higher returns. No surprise, the higher return potential often comes with higher risk. Here the risk picture includes lower liquidity, poor market transparency, regulation issues, and the country risk.

Small-cap stocks: Companies with a market capitalization (cap) of less than $2 billion. They are normally placed in a higher risk category than larger companies.

Mid-cap stocks: Mid-sized companies with a market cap generally from $2 billion to $10 billion.

Large-Cap stocks: Large companies with a market cap over $10 billion.

My ranking from low to high risk: Money markets, bonds (not junk-rated), large-cap stocks, mid-cap stocks, small-cap stocks, and emerging markets.

What is right for you?

Each asset class has different levels of return in relation to the risk that your portfolio is exposed to. Your risk tolerance, time frame, and goals will provide the foundation of the composition of your portfolio. In an attempt to make the asset allocation process easier, investment managers usually create different model portfolios for clients – each model having a different percentage of the asset classes.

The portfolios often range from aggressive to conservative. The aim is to have something for every type of investor risk profile.

Model portfolios

Very aggressive

This is an almost all stocks portfolio. Your goal here is aggressive account value growth over the long term. Being aggressive does normally have a higher amount of risk. This is mostly due to the amount of market volatility that you will be exposed to. If you elect to go with this type of portfolio it is common to see in the short term that your account value will fluctuate widely.

Being emotions free is more important with this model than the others. You should also know that in general, your emotional state is one of the most influential factors in creating investment profits.

Composition: 80%–100% stocks, and maybe minimal amounts of cash or fixed-income securities

Aggressive

Your goal is long-term capital appreciation. The portfolio is mostly equities; therefore, you should expect your account value to have significant fluctuations. Aggressive portfolio investors will often add some fixed income to their portfolio mix.

Composition: 70% stocks, 20%–25% fixed-income securities, and 5%–10% cash

Balanced

Has the ingredients of the aggressive portfolio, but the level of fixed income is noticeably higher when compared to the previous portfolio examples. This is an attempt to provide a balance between income and growth.

If you have a medium level of risk willingness then this strategy is appropriate. The time horizon is three to five years.

Composition: 50% stocks, 35%–40% fixed-income securities, and 10%–15% cash

Conservative

Your goal with a conservative portfolio is very clear: capital preservation and protection of the value of the portfolio. You should also keep in mind that even a conservative strategy still has some exposure to stocks but only in small amounts.

Composition: 70%–75% fixed-income securities, 15%–20% stocks, and 5%–15% cash

Putting it all together

Since I do not know each reader's personal situation, the portfolio suggestions are just that, suggestions, and a guideline to work with. The two most important parameters in creating your portfolio are your time frame and your openness to risk. For example, if you were in a situation where you might need access to your funds on short notice then you would normally have a larger percentage of your investments in short-term fixed-income securities. If short-term liquidity is not an issue for you then your portfolio will have greater exposure to stocks and be lower in fixed income.

Your portfolio will require regular review once you have implemented your strategy. This is to adjust for changes in value of the asset classes. You might be in the situation where you began with a conservative strategy but due to increases in the value of your stocks, you now have a different risk profile from your original goal. To correct this and return to your original, you rebalance your portfolio by selling the portions that have increased. Since we are dealing with investments it's nothing that you have to review daily, but quarterly is a good rule of thumb.

THE RIGHT FUND FOR YOU (MUTUAL, INDEX, AND ETFS)

The actively managed funds that are on the market are really a mixed bag. You will see funds that are popular for a year or maybe even a couple of years but over time, they underperform the market. Enter index funds; they are assembled to track or mirror the composition of a market index. Some examples are the Dow Jones Industrial Average (DJIA) or the Nasdaq Composite. I prefer passive index funds to managed funds with little hesitation and the evidence is convincing:

- The majority of actively managed funds underperform the market and fail to beat index funds.
- The average index fund beats the average funds by a few percentage points.

The "secret" of index funds is that they have a noticeably lower expense ratio. Their cost of doing business is simply lower. Index funds make fewer trades and have smaller staffs, which results in lower expenses. This is possible because the goal of the manager is only to copy the index that the fund is tracking. The reality is you can have actively managed funds that initially outperform an index fund, but after accounting for the expenses from trades and the more expensive management teams ... they lose.

While I prefer index funds to other types, it is important to state that they are *not* risk -free. They are tracking an index; therefore, that index's performance, good or bad, will be reflected in the index fund's performance.

Exchange-traded funds (ETFs)

Another possible component of a diversified portfolio is exchange-traded funds (ETFs). They are securities that track an index similar to the index funds we have covered, but they trade like stocks. An easy way to understand them is to think of ETFs as mutual funds that you can trade as if you are trading a stock.

Why ETFs?

You get the diversification of an index fund, but you have access to leverage (use of margin). This feature is normally not available with mutual funds.

ETFs also offer more accurate pricing in the sense that the price you receive at purchase depends on what point in the day that you buy. For example, if you placed an order to buy in the morning when the fund was trading at a price lower than the closing you will get the lower price. This is in contrast to traditional mutual funds, which are only priced once a day. This means that everyone buying the mutual fund that day gets the same price without taking into consideration what time the purchase was made. This might not be a big deal for a small investor but once the amounts get larger, price sensitivity is more important. Chances are you will be unsatisfied when forced to buy at a price higher than what was available at the exact time that you placed the order.

ALTERNATIVE INVESTMENTS

These are the investments that do not easily fit into the traditional investment categories like bonds and stocks. I include alternatives because people do have a growing interest in them and I also invest in some; therefore, I can write from experience. Alternative investments can include anything from rare wines to gold coins, handbags, and much more. Honestly, I was stunned to know how many people spend considerable amounts of money on handbags primarily for investment purposes. A lot more than I originally thought!

My advice: only buy things you know well and enjoy having around because you might be stuck with them for a long time. The two main challenges with this investment class are liquidity and the difficulty in agreement of the actual value (in most cases). Let us look at this a little deeper. Stocks are liquid for the most part: if you need to sell them you can usually accomplish this within a few seconds or minutes. If you need to determine the value, you can check the last quoted market price. Returning to the world of unique handbags, wines, and so on, you lack a central market; therefore, you are in an over-the-counter environment where it is up to you and your counterpart (the seller) to determine the price. In terms of liquidity, the market for expensive art or watches is clearly not as large as, for example, a popular stock. For those considering these items, you should investigate what is the de facto liquidity. You should also only invest in something that brings you pleasure between sales.

Following my own advice of buying what you know and enjoy, I can get a little crazy with watches. I love and enjoy wearing watches of a certain level, which some might call luxury watches. If you own one of the well-known brands like Rolex you can usually sell them quickly. There was one point in life where I needed to have cash almost instantly and what saved me was two watches from my collection. One I sold in under forty-eight hours, the other took a little longer but it was still relatively liquid. Watches remain my favorite alternative investments, because besides their liquidity, they are easy to transport. I can place one on my wrist or slip one in my pocket without bringing too much attention to myself.

Alternative investments should only be considered after the traditional assets have been taken care of and you have some "play" money. As I mentioned in the introduction of the book, the goal is freedom and we can be creative in how we get there. Alternative investments, similar to the cryptocurrencies that we looked at prior, can be a part of the mix. If your time and/or money is used to acquire assets that create more money it will likely fit in the investing matrix. We can always debate which one is most efficient, but if what you invest in creates more money then at least you are heading in the right direction. Getting the newest smartphone or jeans does not make my list.

ENTREPRENEURSHIP

This is the often-overlooked portion in most investment strategies. As I also stated at the beginning of the book, we will go "beyond the traditional investing strategies" and this is another example. I always recommend that clients have some kind of business, even if it is just a hobby. This section will cover starting a business on the side of your full-time job. With this part-time approach, you can make a gradual transition into entrepreneurship. Given the never-ending uncertainty in the job market, and along with the potential tax advantages, having a side business is a good thing.

I will be transparent and state that this is not a full "how to start a business" section. However, in the following paragraphs, I will share the essential components that must be in place to execute this part of your strategy. My strategies are for those that believe in the authentic version of entrepreneurship: a business with products or services that offers real value to clients. The focus is *not* on raising money and getting funding.

Scalability

Unless your business idea has the ability to scale, keep working on your idea until does. Please resist the urge to start a business until you can figure this out. A quick example for those unfamiliar with the concept of scalable: your business can handle an order for one-thousand units with almost the same ease as an order for one hundred.

Begin part-time

Developing your business while still employed allows you to avoid the stress of economic uncertainty that can come with it. If you end up in the dream situation of having a profitable side business, then you can continue scaling it up to make it your main source of income.

Developing your business muscles

The skills of running a business, unsurprisingly, are developed from deliberate practice and coaching. Taking classes can be useful, but ultimately you will need the coaching or guidance of someone who has or had a profitable business. Done correctly, this will save you time, and in the end money.

Connecting sales and marketing

As you progress with your business, it is important that your emails and website connect with the final or end goal of your potential clients. If you do not know what this goal is, then it is critical that you figure it out as quickly as possible. This knowledge is one of the keys to increasing your sales. My firm, GCMS, specializes in practical capital markets education, but our clients' end goals are either getting a new job or improving their investing knowledge. Therefore, all of our marketing materials focus on these goals. This goes back to the classic business concept of separating a product's benefits from its features.

Here is an excerpt from my book *Your First Start-Up: (Book 2): The Next Steps,* which has been able to help many along the way on their journey to entrepreneurship.

Excerpt from *Your First Start-Up (Book 2): The Next Steps*

Mindset

This topic is always part of my business books because it is more critical than any technology or business strategy. If you do not have the correct mindset for running a scalable business, then all the software in the world will be useless to you.

Well, the obvious question is what is this "mindset" thing? Is it just more fake motivation, make-you-feel-good nonsense of so-called gurus? Not at all, it is simply having the discipline to continue the journey no matter what happens. Many people develop this "continue moving ahead no matter what" mental strength from sports (I did). Luckily, it is *not* the only way to develop this type of strength; one example I love to use is classical musicians. Anyone who has met one knows of the hours they spend perfecting their craft. Many of the people who overcome the rough times that will come from business usually have some other area that helped them develop this trait. Remember, that even the smallest steps still move you forward.

Success

A key part of mindset is determining for yourself what success is for *you*. Avoid the trap of copying other people's views of success. For you, it might be income to supplement what you earn at your job or it could be to replace the job altogether. Another person might have a goal that is more philanthropic, for example, making a change in society that has nothing to do with making a financial profit. Please keep in mind that even a nonprofit organization is not the same as for-loss. Even these organizations need and use many principles of the start-up world.

Once you have determined what success is for you, then the steps needed to accomplish it must be taken. It has been told to me many times and it remains true: "We do not step into or just arrive into the future; we create it from what we are doing today." What you harvest in six months or six years, fairly or unfairly, is mostly from what you are planting now. I suggest that you ask yourself, "What am I planting?"

NEXT STEPS

When You Are Ready To Begin – Contact me

I sincerely hope that this practical book was of benefit to you. However, I also realize that books do have limitations and for those who would like more hands-on coaching, please contact me here: www.gcmsonline.info, where I can respond to you.

If you have not read any of my other books, then I invite you to do so because they have valuable lessons that will be helpful to your development as an investor.

Some of my other books that are most relevant to investing include:

Your First Start-Up

Asset Class Mastery

The Next Level of Cryptocurrency Investing

ABOUT THE AUTHOR

Wayne **Walker** is the director of a global capital markets education and consulting firm, gcmsonline.info. He has several years' experience in leading and coaching teams of investment advisors and has managed top-performing teams in the private client group based on benchmark earnings (BME). Wayne has trained traders of the Citi-FX Pro program in London. He also developed the "Trading Rights" program at Saxo Bank, which investment advisors were required to complete before being allowed to trade. He is a certified trader by Markets in Financial Instrument Directive (MiFID) EU and is qualified to advise "A" clients.

Wayne is a frequently invited guest capital markets commentator on several international TV and radio programs.

Wayne holds multiple certifications and has worked in the following positions:

- Director-Founder, (GCMS) Global Capital Market Solutions, Denmark
- Author of *Reality-Based Trading Guide,* (used in our classes at Copenhagen Business School & other universities in the EU)
- Manager, Sales Trading, North America & Middle East, Saxo Bank, Denmark
- B.sc, State University of New York, College at Buffalo, USA
- NASD Series 3 – License to trade & advise on futures contracts in the US market

- ACI (Financial Markets) Dealing Certificate with Distinction (highest level), France

- Trained in Bloomberg & UBS Bank's FX Options quoting software

www.ingramcontent.com/pod-product-compliance
Lightning Source LLC
Chambersburg PA
CBHW021914170526
45157CB00005B/2068